from SEA TO SHINING SEA

COLORADO

By Dennis Brindell Fradin

CONSULTANTS

David Fridtjof Halaas, Ph.D., State Historian, Colorado Historical Society

Robert L. Hillerich, Ph.D., Professor Emeritus, Bowling Green State University;
Consultant, Pinellas County Schools, Florida

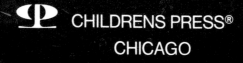

CHILDRENS PRESS®
CHICAGO

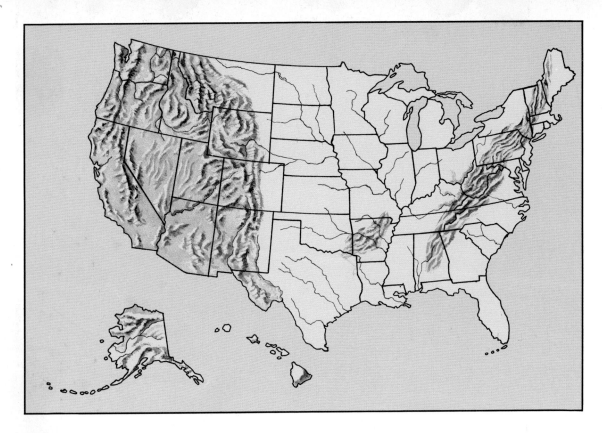

Colorado is one of the six Rocky Mountain states. The other Rocky Mountain states are Idaho, Montana, Nevada, Utah, and Wyoming.

For Bob Handler

Front cover picture: aspen trees and the peaks of the San Juan Mountains; page 1: the Ruby Range Mountains in Gunnison; back cover: lupine on Grand Mesa, Grand Mesa National Forest

Project Editor: Joan Downing
Design Director: Karen Kohn
Research Assistant: Judith Bloom Fradin
Typesetting: Graphic Connections, Inc.
Engraving: Liberty Photoengraving

Library of Congress Cataloging-in-Publication Data

Fradin, Dennis B.
  Colorado/ by Dennis Brindell Fradin.
    p.   cm. — (From sea to shining sea)
  Includes index.
  Summary: An overview of the Centennial State,
introducing its history, geography, industries, sites of
interest, and famous people.
  ISBN 0-516-03806-0
  1. Colorado—Juvenile literature. I. Title. II. Series:
Fradin, Dennis B. From sea to shining sea.
F776.3.F68   1993   93-2648
978.8—dc20   CIP
                                           AC

Skiers on a chair lift

Table of Contents

Introducing the Centennial State

Colorado is a large state in the western United States. It is shaped like a rectangle. *Colorado* is a Spanish word meaning "red." The state was named for the Colorado River. This river flows through red canyons. Colorado is nicknamed the "Centennial State." It became a state in 1876. In that year, the United States had its centennial—its 100th birthday.

The Rocky Mountains cover much of western Colorado. Pikes Peak is a very famous mountain. It is in the Colorado Rockies. Colorado's mountains attract huge numbers of skiers.

Colorado was the site of a gold rush in 1858-59. The state is still a mining leader. Its farmers produce cattle, sheep, and wheat. Workers in Colorado cities make many kinds of goods. They include computers, beer, and medical instruments.

Colorado is special in other ways. Where are coins with a "D" on them made? Where do the Nuggets play basketball, the Rockies play baseball, and the Broncos play football? Where is there a town named Dinosaur? The answer to these questions is: Colorado!

Only seven states are larger than Colorado. They are Alaska, Texas, California, Montana, New Mexico, Arizona, and Nevada.

A picture map of Colorado

Overleaf: Maroon Bells, in White River National Forest

"Where the Columbines Grow"

"WHERE THE COLUMBINES GROW"

Colorado covers 104,091 square miles. Seven states border Colorado. Wyoming and part of Nebraska are to the north. Part of Nebraska and Kansas are to the east. Oklahoma and New Mexico lie to the south. Arizona touches Colorado's southwest corner. Utah is to the west.

Colorado is one of the Rocky Mountain states. The Rockies are North America's biggest mountain chain. They cover most of Colorado's western half. Most of Colorado's mining is done there. The Rockies help make Colorado the highest of the fifty states. Colorado's average height is 6,800 feet. That's 1.25 miles above sea level. Mount Elbert is Colorado's highest mountain. It is 14,433 feet tall.

Colorado's eastern two-fifths is mostly smooth and flat. This area is part of the Great Plains. Most of Colorado's farming takes place there. Between the Rockies and the Great Plains stand Colorado's largest cities. They include Denver, Aurora, Arvada, Lakewood, Westminster, Colorado Springs, Boulder, Fort Collins, Loveland, Greeley, and Pueblo.

Elk are among the animals that live in Colorado.

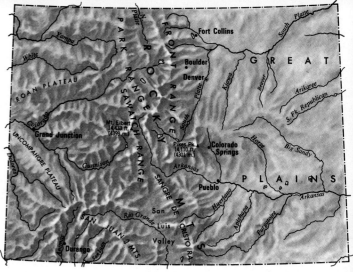

TOPOGRAPHY

| Below Sea Level | 100 m. 328 ft. | 200 m. 656 ft. | 500 m. 1,640 ft. | 1,000 m. 3,281 ft. | 2,000 m. 6,562 ft. | 5,000 m. 16,404 ft. |

WOODS AND WILDLIFE

One-third of Colorado is forested. The blue spruce is the state tree. This tree is widely used as a Christmas tree. Aspens are common. Other trees in Colorado include pines, firs, and cottonwoods.

Wildflowers color Colorado's mountain meadows. The Rocky Mountain columbine has blue and white petals. It is the state flower. Colorado's state song is "Where the Columbines Grow." Cactus plants grow in dry parts of Colorado.

Bighorn sheep climb through the mountains. These wild sheep are the state animal. Mountain goats and mountain lions also roam the highlands. Plenty of deer and elk live in Colorado. There are also black bears, beavers, foxes, coyotes, and prairie

Above left: A field of wildflowers in Gunnison National Forest

Coyotes are in the dog family. Prairie dogs are a kind of squirrel.

9

Autumn at Mount Sopris

Bald eagles can be seen in Colorado.

dogs. The lark bunting is the state bird. Hummingbirds suck nectar from the columbine flowers. Eagles soar above Colorado.

CLIMATE

Colorado has a dry, cool, and sunny climate. The Rockies are cooler than the plains, though. Denver lies where the mountains meet the plains. In the summer, Denver's temperature is often around 75 degrees Fahrenheit. At the same time, the plains might be 95 degrees Fahrenheit. The mountains might be 55 degrees Fahrenheit. Denver's winter temperatures are often around 40 degrees Fahrenheit. Meanwhile, it could be 50 degrees

Fahrenheit on the plains. In the mountains, it could be 10 degrees Fahrenheit.

Long dry periods called droughts have hurt Colorado's farming at times. Yet, the state is also subject to rainstorms and snowstorms. On April 14-15, 1921, 76 inches of snow fell at Silver Lake, just northeast of Silverton. This is the record twenty-four-hour snowfall for all of North America.

The Silver Lake snowfall was equal to the height of a 6-foot, 4-inch person.

Rivers and Lakes

Another of Colorado's nicknames is the "Mother of Rivers." No other state gives rise to as many major rivers. The Colorado River begins in the northern Colorado Rockies. It flows 1,450 miles to the Gulf of California. The Rio Grande begins its nearly 1,900-mile journey in Colorado. The Arkansas, North Platte, South Platte, and San Juan rivers also start in Colorado.

Hundreds of natural lakes reflect the blue Colorado sky. The largest is Grand Lake. But it doesn't even cover a square mile. Colorado's largest lakes were made by damming rivers. The John Martin and Blue Mesa reservoirs are two such lakes in Colorado. Their waters run through ditches and canals to towns and farms.

Green Lake, in Gunnison National Forest

From Ancient Times Until Today

From Ancient Times Until Today

Dinosaurs once roamed Colorado. Tyrannosaurus rex and Apatosaurus lived there. Tyrannosaurus rex ate other dinosaurs. But Apatosaurus ate plants. Stegosaurus also lived in Colorado. This dinosaur had bony plates along its back. In 1991, Stegosaurus was named Colorado's state fossil.

American Indians

American Indians (Native Americans) reached Colorado at least 20,000 years ago. Tools and weapons made by these early Indians have been found. About 2,000 years ago, Basket Maker Indians lived in Colorado. They made baskets, clothing, and sandals from grasses and branches.

About 1,000 years ago, the Anasazi built homes along cliffs. They were called Cliff Dwellers. Their buildings sometimes had hundreds of rooms. They were much like today's apartment buildings.

More recently, several Indian tribes lived in Colorado. Arapahos, Cheyennes, and Comanches hunted buffalo on the plains. They made tepees and

Opposite: Anasazi Indian ruins, Mesa Verde National Park

Anasazi pottery at Mesa Verde National Park

clothing with buffalo skins. The Utes hunted deer and gathered berries in the mountain valleys.

EUROPEAN AND AMERICAN EXPLORERS

Spaniards were the first non-Indians in Colorado. They came searching for gold in the late 1500s. In 1706, Juan de Ulibarri arrived. He claimed Colorado for Spain. France had claimed the region in 1682. Neither country settled Colorado, though.

In 1776, the United States declared its independence from England. The new country's first states were in the East. But soon American explorers headed West. Zebulon Pike reached Colorado in 1806. Pikes Peak was named for him.

Stephen H. Long arrived in 1820. He became the first white American to discover Longs Peak. It was named for him. Dr. Edwin James traveled with Long. James made the first-known climb all the way up Pikes Peak.

MOUNTAIN MEN AND FIRST SETTLEMENTS

Mountain men also entered Colorado in the early 1800s. They searched for beaver and other furs. Some trapped the animals. Others traded with the

Major Stephen H. Long

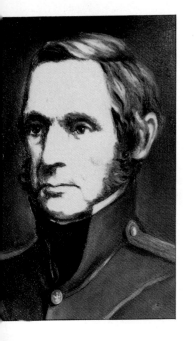

Indians for the furs. The furs were used to make hats and other clothing.

Bent's Fort

Meanwhile, Colorado was slowly coming under United States control. The young country bought some French lands in 1803. This was called the Louisiana Purchase. It included Colorado's eastern half. Spain still claimed western Colorado. But in 1821, this claim passed to Mexico. In that year, Mexico broke free of Spain.

Jim Beckwourth

Colorado's first permanent non-Indian settlement was completed in 1833-34. It was a trading post called Bent's Fort. William Bent managed it. He was among Colorado's first white settlers. Famed mountain man Kit Carson worked at Bent's Fort. Jim Beckwourth, a black mountain man, also worked in Colorado. In 1842, Beckwourth helped found a trading post. That was the start of Pueblo, Colorado.

In the 1840s, the United States wanted land that was claimed by Mexico. In 1846, the United States and Mexico went to war. The United States won the Mexican War in 1848. Mexico gave up a large piece of land. It included western Colorado. All of Colorado was then governed by the United States.

GOLD RUSH, POPULATION BOOM, AND STATEHOOD

At first, Colorado was just land claimed by the United States. To become a state, Colorado first had to be made a territory. But this required several thousand settlers.

Many Colorado miners used surefooted burros to carry their gear.

In the 1850s, some Mexican people came to Colorado from New Mexico. They raised sheep and planted crops. They also founded towns such as Conejos and San Luis. Yet Colorado still had only a few hundred people. Then, something happened that caused great growth.

In 1858, William Green Russell found gold. Word spread that gold had been discovered. Thousands of people rushed to the region. Denver was begun where the discovery was made.

Also in 1858, Julia Archibald Holmes became the first woman to climb Pikes Peak.

A lucky few made big gold strikes. In 1859, George Jackson and John Gregory each made a great strike. Their strikes were west of Denver. Central City was started where John Gregory found gold. Golden, Boulder, and Colorado City were also begun in 1859.

Many who didn't find gold stayed and set up stores. These people also obtained gold. Sometimes miners paid for supplies with "pinches" of gold dust. A pinch was an amount held between the thumb and index finger. A pinch of gold dust was worth twenty-five cents. An egg cost one dollar, or four pinches of gold dust. A sack of potatoes cost fifteen dollars. That was sixty pinches of gold dust. Prices were high because goods were shipped overland to Colorado.

Today, many abandoned gold mines like this one can be seen in Colorado.

William Byers

Clara Brown

Women also helped build Colorado in the 1850s. In 1858, German-born Catherine Murat became the first white woman to enter Denver. She was called the "Mother of Colorado." Murat flew the first American flag in Denver. She made it from clothing.

In 1859, Elizabeth and William Byers came to Denver. That year, they founded Colorado's first newspaper. Elizabeth named it the *Rocky Mountain News.* The paper is still published today. Clara Brown was a former slave. She also arrived in 1859. Brown was among Colorado's first black women settlers. She bought property in and near Central City. Brown is remembered mainly for nursing the sick.

By 1860, Colorado's population was 34,277. The United States Congress made Colorado a territory in 1861. Coloradans then had a territorial governor. They also sent a delegate to the United States Congress.

During that time, the miners and settlers pushed the Indians off their land. In November 1864, Colorado troops attacked an Indian village on Sand Creek. They murdered about 150 Arapahos and Cheyennes. The Indians fought fiercely after that to hold their land. But by 1881, most of them had been driven from Colorado. The Utes were moved to a reservation in southwestern Colorado.

In 1870, the railroads reached Colorado. Trains brought in thousands of new settlers. United States lawmakers saw that the time for statehood had arrived. Colorado was made the thirty-eighth state on August 1, 1876. The United States had held its centennial a month earlier. Colorado became known as the "Centennial State."

SILVER, MORE GOLD, OIL, AND WATER

Colorado's path to statehood had been paved with gold. By the 1870s, however, the gold seemed to be

By 1881, most of Colorado's Indians had been driven out of the state.

Horace Tabor (above) and Elizabeth "Baby" Doe Tabor (below)

running out. In 1878, rich silver strikes were made in Colorado. This set off a "silver rush." Leadville and Aspen were two silver-mining towns.

Horace Tabor earned $10 million from his Matchless Mine near Leadville. He became known as the "Silver King." Tabor used his money to build opera houses in Leadville and Denver. In 1883, he married Elizabeth "Baby" Doe. They lived in a Denver mansion.

Then, in 1893, the price of silver dropped. Silver miners were thrown out of work. Mine owners, including Horace Tabor, went broke. Tabor ended his days as Denver's postmaster. He died in 1899. Elizabeth moved to a shack near the Matchless Mine. She died there in 1935 from cold and hunger. This rags-to-riches-to-rags story became famous. An opera about the Tabors came out in 1956. It is called *The Ballad of Baby Doe*.

While silver mining was going badly, a second gold rush started. In 1890, Bob Womack, a cowboy, found gold. It was in a cow pasture. Womack sold his claim for $300. He made a bad deal. Half a billion dollars in gold was mined from the pasture. The town of Cripple Creek grew near the gold field. By 1900, Cripple Creek was the world's second-leading gold-mining center.

In the early 1900s, oil became important to Colorado. It was called "black gold." Oil is made into gasoline. The country needed gasoline to run a new invention, the car.

Placer miners at the Cripple Creek gold field, 1893

Although Colorado became a big oil-producing state, it had little water. Water was needed for the dry farmlands of eastern Colorado. Many irrigation projects were built in the early 1900s. They carried water to farms by canals and ditches. By 1909, Colorado had more irrigated land than any other state. These water projects helped Coloradans grow sugar beets and other crops. A southeast Colorado town was named Sugar City. Sugar was packaged there.

WORLD WARS, DEPRESSION, AND COLD WAR

In 1917, the United States entered World War I (1914-1918). About 43,000 Coloradans served in

About 1,000 Coloradans died in World War I.

This dust storm hit Prowers County in eastern Colorado on March 21, 1937.

the army and navy. Colorado's crops and mining goods also helped win the war.

During the 1930s, drought hit much of the country. Colorado's fields dried up. Great windstorms sent the dirt swirling. Parts of eastern Colorado were in an area called the Dust Bowl.

This happened at a bad time. The 1930s were the years of the Great Depression. Many businesses closed in Colorado and in the other states. Mining suffered. Thousands of Colorado farmers and ranchers lost their land. In Colorado's cities, people stood in lines for food.

World War II (1939-1945) helped end the Great Depression. The United States entered the war in 1941. Colorado's factories sprang back to life. In Denver, they made weapons for the war. The country needed Colorado's oil. Fort Carson opened in Colorado during the war. About 140,000 Colorado men and women were in uniform. About 3,000 of them died helping to win the war.

Fort Carson was named for Kit Carson.

After World War II ended, the "Cold War" (1948-1989) began. This was not a shooting war. Instead, the United States and Russia greatly feared each other. Both countries built bombs and missiles for protection.

Colorado became a major defense center. In 1957, a United States-Canada program began. It was to guard against Russian air attacks. It is called

These troops were among the 140,000 Colorado men and women who were in uniform during World War II.

NORAD. That stands for North American Aerospace Defense Command. NORAD's command center was completed near Colorado Springs in 1966. It lies 1,200 feet underground within Cheyenne Mountain. Radar reports go to the command center. They would show if an air attack was coming.

GROWTH, PROBLEMS, AND NEW LEADERS

Colorado was one of the fastest-growing states from 1950 to 1975. Its population doubled to 2.5 million during that time. Many of the newcomers worked in manufacturing or tourism.

Defense companies moved to Colorado. They made missiles and other weapons. Companies that made scientific instruments also arrived.

Meanwhile, tourism was growing in Colorado. Aspen, the old silver-mining town, became a leading ski resort. Other ski resorts were built in Vail and Steamboat Springs. By the 1960s, Colorado was one of the world's leading ski areas.

Colorado's growing population and businesses created problems. Pollution from cars and factories dirtied the air. Coloradans are now working to clean the air over their large cities.

The many outdoor activities enjoyed in Colorado have brought people to the state.

Water is another big issue. Colorado can't supply all the water that everyone wants. The Colorado River faces problems because of this demand for water. The river provides water to seven states and Mexico. But the dams and canals along the river have hurt its natural flow. Droughts in the late 1980s and early 1990s lowered the river's level. Colorado and neighboring states have argued over who has rights to the water. Obtaining enough water while saving its rivers is a great Colorado challenge.

Colorado's new leaders must solve these problems. In 1983, Federico Peña became the first Hispanic mayor of Denver. In 1993, Peña became President Bill Clinton's secretary of transportation. Wellington Webb was elected Denver's first black mayor in 1991. Another first came in 1992. Coloradans elected Ben Nighthorse Campbell to the United States Senate. Campbell became the first American Indian senator from Colorado.

The Winterskol Parade in Aspen

Senator Ben Nighthorse Campbell

25

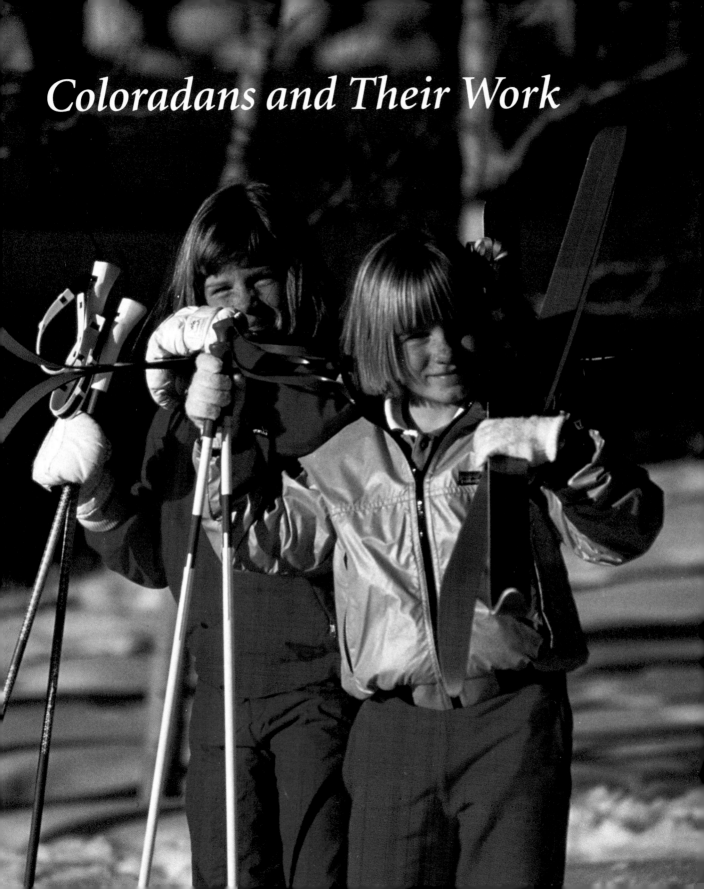

Coloradans and Their Work

COLORADANS AND THEIR WORK

Colorado is average in population size. The United States Census counted 3,294,394 Coloradans in 1990. Twenty-five states have more people. Twenty-four have fewer.

Nine of every ten Coloradans are white. Small numbers of black, American Indian, and Asian people also live in Colorado. The state has one of the country's largest Hispanic populations. About 500,000 people of Spanish-speaking background live there. Mexican people were among Colorado's first settlers. Many cities hold a Mexican festival called Cinco de Mayo. There is Mexican dancing and music. Chili and other Mexican dishes are served.

A Southern Ute woman etching designs into pottery

Soccer players at the U. S. Olympic Training Complex in Colorado Springs

Colorado ranks high in ways that make life good. Coloradans tend to be outdoors people. This may account for their good health. The average Coloradan lives more than seventy-five years. That's longer than people in all but a few states. Coloradans also rank high in income. Each Coloradan earns an average of nearly $20,000 a year. Coloradans are also well educated. Nearly nine Colorado adults in ten have finished high school.

One in four has finished college. Few states have people as well educated.

COLORADANS AT WORK

Over 1.5 million Coloradans have jobs. That is about half the state's people. Service work is Colorado's leading type of job. The state's 380,000 service workers include nurses and doctors. People who work at ski resorts and motels are counted, too.

About 360,000 Coloradans sell goods. Another 270,000 do government work. The air force and NORAD employ many of these government workers.

Almost 200,000 Coloradans make products. Colorado is a top maker of scientific equipment. Martin Marietta of Denver helped launch the space age. This company's rockets have sent spacecraft to Venus and Mars. Medical supplies are also made in Colorado. They include heart monitors and artificial blood. A Colorado firm makes parts for air bags in cars. Another firm makes Waterpiks. People use them to clean their teeth.

Colorado is a major packer of meats and other foods. Only Texas brews more beer than Colorado.

These vacationers are enjoying a llama carriage ride in Aspen. People who work at ski resorts are part of Colorado's service industry.

The famous Coors Brewery is in Golden. It is the world's biggest brewery. Colorado ranks among the top ten states at making computers. It also makes office equipment. Luggage and skiing and camping equipment are other Colorado products.

About 50,000 Coloradans work on farms and ranches. Colorado is a leader at raising beef cattle, sheep, and horses. Hay, wheat, and corn are leading crops. Lettuce, cherries, pears, plums, and potatoes are other important crops.

Almost 20,000 Coloradans work at mining. They make their state a mining leader. Oil, natural gas, and coal are now the state's main mining products. Colorado is also a big miner of gold, silver, and uranium.

Above: Barley being harvested

Only three states have more sheep than Colorado. Only five have more horses.

A Trip Through the
Centennial State

A Trip Through the Centennial State

About 11 million people visit Colorado each year. Many come to ski. People also come to explore Colorado's Indian ruins. Others visit Denver and other big cities.

Pages 30-31: The Denver skyline

Denver: The Mile High City

Denver is a good place to start a Colorado trip. The city is on the South Platte River. It is a few miles east of the Rockies in central Colorado. Denver has about 470,000 people. It is Colorado's biggest city. Denver suburbs such as Lakewood, Arvada, and Westminster are good-sized cities, too. Half of all Coloradans live in the Denver area.

Denver has been Colorado's capital since 1867. State lawmakers work in the capitol in downtown Denver. Horace Tabor, the "Silver King," laid the capitol's cornerstone. That happened on July 4, 1890. Denver is nicknamed the "Mile High City." The thirteenth step at the capitol is 5,280 feet high. That's exactly 1 mile above sea level.

The United States Mint in Denver is near the capitol. The United States government makes 5 bil-

The United States Mint in Denver

lion coins a year there. Coins stamped with a "D" come from the mint in Denver. Visitors can see how the coins are made.

The capitol

The Molly Brown House is a Denver landmark. Molly was on the *Titanic* when it hit an iceberg in 1912. Fifteen hundred people sank with the ship. But Molly survived and rowed other passengers to safety. "I'm unsinkable!" she explained. A movie, *The Unsinkable Molly Brown,* was made about her. Today, Molly's house has displays of Denver and Brown family history.

The Denver Art Museum

Denver has many fine museums. The Denver Art Museum has a collection of American Indian

33

artwork. The Museum of Western Art has works by great western artists. The Denver Museum of Natural History displays dinosaur fossils. The Colorado History Museum has displays on the history of the state.

Denver is the state's pro sports center. The Denver Broncos are the football team. The Denver Nuggets play basketball there. In 1993, the Colorado Rockies began playing major-league baseball in Denver.

Twice a year, Denver hosts the Colorado Indian Market. It is one of the country's largest Native American art shows. Indian artists from about 100 tribes attend. They display woven blankets, handmade dolls, pottery, and artworks.

Denver has enjoyed a recent building boom. The Denver Center for the Performing Arts added 2,800 seats. It hosts plays and concerts. Denver International Airport opened in 1993.

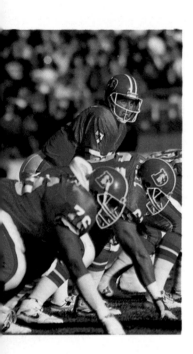

The Denver Broncos during a football game

OTHER CENTRAL COLORADO CITIES

Aurora is just east of Denver. Only 2,000 people lived in Aurora fifty years ago. An oil boom in the 1970s and 1980s helped Aurora grow. Today, Aurora has over 220,000 people.

Boulder is to the northwest of Denver. The town was named for the rocks, or boulders, in the area. Boulder is the home of the state's biggest school. That is the University of Colorado. The University of Colorado Buffaloes won the country's 1990 college football title.

The National Institute of Standards and Technology is in Boulder. It decides exact time and exact weight. An atomic clock can be seen there. It keeps the exact time. The National Center for Atmospheric Research is also in Boulder. Its scientists study thunderstorms. They also study how storms on the sun affect earth's climate.

Northeast of Boulder is Greeley. New York newspaperman Horace Greeley visited Colorado in 1859. He felt that the West had a golden future. He popularized the phrase "Go West, young man!" In 1870, Nathan Meeker founded Union Colony. The town was planned by Horace Greeley. It was later named for him. Today, Nathan Meeker's home is a Greeley landmark.

Fort Collins is northwest of Greeley. It is home to Colorado State University. Thousands of veterinarians have been trained at this school.

Colorado Springs is south of Denver. The town was begun in 1871. It was named for nearby

A football game between Colorado State and the University of Colorado

The University of Colorado in Boulder

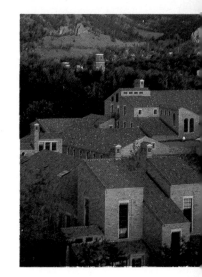

Gymnasts training at the USOTC

Pikes Peak and the Kissing Camels Rock

springs, or bubbling water. Colorado Springs is now the state's second-biggest city.

The United States Olympic Training Complex (USOTC) is in Colorado Springs. Many of the country's Olympic athletes have trained there. Colorado Springs is also home to two halls of fame. The Pro Rodeo Hall of Fame honors rodeo stars. Great skaters are honored at the World Figure Skating Hall of Fame.

A wonderland of red rocks is in Colorado Springs. It is called the Garden of the Gods. The rocks have such names as the Sleeping Giant and the Kissing Camels. The Ute Indians say that the rocks

were once giants. The Great Spirit turned them to stone because they invaded Ute lands.

The United States Air Force Academy is near Colorado Springs. This famous college trains young people for air force careers.

Pueblo is the southernmost of Colorado's big cities. With nearly 100,000 people, it is the state's fifth-largest city. The El Pueblo Museum is a highlight of Pueblo. It has displays on Pueblo's Indians and mountain men. Pueblo is also the site of the State Fairgrounds. The Colorado State Fair is held there each summer. It features a rodeo and horse shows.

The Garden of the Gods

A United States Air Force Academy parade

Highlights of Western Colorado

The Rockies begin just west of the central cities. Pikes Peak is only a few miles west of Colorado Springs. Cars climb the 14,110-foot peak along Pikes Peak Highway. A railroad also goes up the mountain. Some people ride horses to the top.

In 1893, Katharine Lee Bates went up Pikes Peak. The view inspired her to write a poem. It began: "O beautiful, for spacious skies, for amber waves of grain . . ." Her poem was set to music. It became the lovely song "America the Beautiful."

Colorado has fifty-six of the country's ninety-one named peaks that are over 14,000 feet tall. Coloradans call these peaks "fourteeners." Most

Pikes Peak

Longs Peak and the Front Range, Rocky Mountain National Park

have good trails to the top. A trail leads up 14,433-foot Mount Elbert, Colorado's highest peak.

Several well-known ski areas are north of Pikes Peak. Each year, Vail and Aspen host the World Cup Ski Racing Competitions. Nearby Arapaho Mountain has North America's highest ski area. It is 12,450 feet high.

To the east is Rocky Mountain National Park. Longs Peak is the highest of this park's many mountains. Bighorn sheep, black bears, deer, and elk roam through the park. Peregrine falcons fly about. They are the world's fastest birds. These falcons can reach speeds of 220 miles per hour.

The Rockies have some "ghost towns." These were once booming mining towns. When the gold

Colorado has more than 11,000 miles of mountain hiking trails—one-tenth of the country's total.

Left: A cabin at Capitol City, a ghost town
Right: Winter fireworks over Aspen

or silver ran out, the people moved away. They left empty towns behind. Colorado's ghost towns include St. Elmo, Eldora, and Gold Hill.

Steamboat Springs is very much alive. This is a famous resort town. It is west of Rocky Mountain National Park. The town was named for a bubbling spring. The water from it sounded like a steamboat whistle. People come to Steamboat Springs to bathe in the warm spring waters. It is also a popular skiing area.

Grand Junction has almost 30,000 people. It is western Colorado's largest city. Grand Junction lies near the center of far western Colorado. The

The Dinosaur Quarry Museum at Dinosaur National Monument

Dinosaur Valley Museum there has dinosaur and other fossil exhibits. Colorado National Monument is outside Grand Junction. This area is known for its deep, red-rock canyons.

More than fifty kinds of dinosaurs lived in far western Colorado. Many dinosaur fossils have come from Rabbit Valley. That is not far from Grand Junction. The fossils include Apatosaurus and Stegosaurus bones. Northwest Colorado even has a town called Dinosaur. It is near Dinosaur National Monument. This parkland where dinosaurs once roamed is in both Colorado and Utah.

Colorado's southwest point is part of the "Four Corners." This is the only place in the country where four states meet. Their corners touch at one point. Anasazi Indians once lived in the Four Corners region. Mesa Verde National Park is in southwest Colorado. It has 800-year-old Anasazi cliff dwellings. One, Cliff Palace, has more than 200 rooms. Visitors reach the cliff dwellings by stairways and ladders. The Anasazi left Mesa Verde suddenly around the year 1300. A drought may have forced them to move away.

Northeast of Mesa Verde is Great Sand Dunes National Monument. It is in the south-central part of the state. North America's tallest sand dunes

The states of Colorado, Utah, Arizona, and New Mexico touch at Four Corners Area Monument.

A hiker at the Cliff Palace, Mesa Verde

*Left: Royal Gorge
Right: Great Sand
Dunes National
Monument*

*The Arkansas River
cut Royal Gorge
Canyon over the ages.*

stand there. Wind piled up the dunes over thousands of years. Some dunes are 700 feet tall. This is the height of a seventy-story building. Some people ski or sled down the dunes. They do this when there is no snow.

Northeast of the dunes is Royal Gorge. This famous canyon is near Canon City. People cross the canyon on the world's highest suspension bridge above water. The Royal Gorge Bridge hangs 1,053 feet above the Arkansas River. Visitors can also take the world's steepest incline railway to the canyon's bottom. That is 1,550 feet down.

HIGHLIGHTS OF EASTERN COLORADO

Farms that grow grain cover much of eastern Colorado. Wheat is a grain that looks amber (golden-brown) when ripe. The wheat fields ripple like waves in the wind. This is what Katharine Lee Bates meant by "amber waves of grain."

Wheat is used to make bread, cakes, and cookies.

La Junta is southeast Colorado's largest town. It has just over 8,000 people. The Koshare Indian Kiva Museum is found there. Visitors can see jewelry, beads, and baskets. They were made by people from many Indian tribes.

Bent's Old Fort is near La Junta. Colorado's first permanent non-Indian settlement has been

A Conestoga wagon at Bent's Old Fort

rebuilt. The fort looks much as it did in 1833-34. Visitors can see how mountain men such as Kit Carson lived and worked.

Carson's name is honored in eastern Colorado. North of La Junta is a town called Kit Carson. The Kit Carson Museum there has the famed mountain man's six-shooter. Eastern Colorado also has Kit Carson County. Burlington is its county seat. It has an area called Old Town with 100-year-old buildings. There is a sod house at Old Town, too. The Colorado plains have stretches where no trees grow. Some pioneer families cut chunks of the ground into blocks. They used these dirt and grass blocks to build sod homes. Visitors can learn about Colorado's plains settlers at Old Town.

Julesburg is in Colorado's northeast corner. It was a stop for the Pony Express. This was a mail service during 1860 and 1861. Fourteen-year-old William Cody signed up as a Pony Express rider in Julesburg. Later, he became a famous buffalo hunter. People called him "Buffalo Bill." The Fort Sedgwick Depot Museum is in Julesburg. Visitors can learn about Buffalo Bill and the Pony Express there.

East of Julesburg, near Sterling, is Pawnee National Grassland. It is a good place to end a

Colorado trip. Antelope, coyotes, and prairie dogs live on the grasslands. East and West Pawnee buttes rise above the grasslands. They are 300-foot sandstone towers. East Pawnee Butte was once a lookout point for Indians. Some people say that the buttes look like stone ships.

Soapweed yucca plants such as the ones shown in these two pictures grow in the Pawnee National Grasslands.

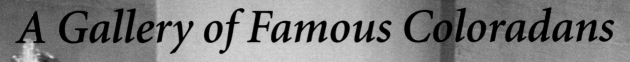
A Gallery of Famous Coloradans

FLORENCE RENA SABIN 1871-1953
DOCTOR OF MEDICINE

A GALLERY OF FAMOUS COLORADANS

Opposite: A statue of Florence Rena Sabin

Many Coloradans have made their marks on American life. They include Indian chiefs, scientists, and athletes. **Black Kettle** (1801-1868) was born on the Great Plains. This famous Cheyenne chief lived in Colorado and other plains states. He led the Indians who camped on Colorado's Sand Creek in 1864. He raised a white flag over his tepee. This was a sign of peace. Soldiers attacked anyway. They killed about 150 Indians. Black Kettle escaped. Four years later, troops under Lt. Col. George Custer attacked Black Kettle's camp in Oklahoma. The soldiers shot and killed Black Kettle and his wife. They also killed about 100 other Cheyennes.

Ute chief **Ouray** (1820-1880) also believed in peace with the whites. Ouray settled arguments between his people and the settlers. He worked out a treaty that gave the Utes land in southwest Colorado. A Colorado town and county were named after him.

Chipeta (1843-1924) was Ouray's wife. She was called the "Laughing Maiden of the Utes." In 1879, Utes killed Nathan Meeker at a reservation.

Ute chief Ouray

John Evans

Emily Griffith

He had founded Greeley. Then the United States government sent him to run a Ute reservation. The Utes kidnapped Meeker's wife, daughter, and several other people. Chipeta convinced the Indians to free the captives. The Ute Indian Museum is at Montrose. Chipeta once lived on the farm. Her grave is there today.

Barney Ford (1824-1902) was born a slave in Virginia. He ran away from slavery and came to Colorado in 1860. Ford became a Denver hotel owner. He provided money and jobs for runaway and freed slaves. Ford also started Colorado's first classes for black adults.

John Evans (1814-1897) was born in Ohio. He became a doctor and teacher. Evans was appointed Colorado's territorial governor in 1862. Two years later, he founded the University of Denver. In 1870, he built the Denver Pacific Railroad. This linked Colorado to the rest of the country.

Emily Griffith (1868-1947) was also an Ohio native. She became a Denver teacher. Griffith founded Denver's Opportunity School in 1916. It offered free classes for adults who wanted to improve their lives. Now called the Emily Griffith Opportunity School, it is still open.

Douglas Fairbanks in his role as Robin Hood

Florence Sabin (1871-1953) was born in Central City. She became a doctor and scientist. Dr. Sabin studied diseases, blood, and how babies develop. Her work led to longer, healthier lives for people. Each state has a statue of at least one person in the U.S. Capitol. Colorado's statue is of Dr. Florence Sabin.

Willard Libby (1908-1980) was born in Grand Valley. He became a scientist. Dr. Libby discovered how to tell the age of very old objects. This is called radiocarbon dating. He won the 1960 Nobel Prize for his work.

Two great stars of the early movies were Coloradans. **Douglas Fairbanks** (1883-1939) was

Willard Libby

born in Denver. He made action movies. They included *The Three Musketeers* and *Robin Hood*. **Lon Chaney** (1883-1930) was born in Colorado Springs. He was called the "Man of a Thousand Faces." With makeup, Chaney could totally change how he looked. He starred in *The Phantom of the Opera*.

Jack Dempsey (1895-1983) was born in Manassa. He became a great heavyweight boxing champion (1919-1926). He was called the "Manassa Mauler." Dempsey knocked out more than twenty-five men in the first round of fights. No other boxer has matched this record.

Jack Dempsey

Another Colorado athlete is **Rich Gossage.** He was born in Colorado Springs in 1951. He became a great baseball pitcher. "Goose" Gossage has saved more than 300 games. That places him high on the all-time saves list.

Author **Mary Coyle Chase** (1907-1981) was born in Denver. She wrote the play *Harvey.* It is about a man whose friend is an invisible, 6-foot-tall rabbit. In 1945, Chase won a Pulitzer Prize for her play.

Mary Coyle Chase

Henry John Deutschendorf, Jr., was born in New Mexico in 1943. He changed his name to John Denver because he so loved the Mile High

John Denver

On the football field, Byron White (above) was known as "Whizzer" White.

Patricia Schroeder

City. John Denver settled in Aspen. He became a famous singer and composer. His songs include "Rocky Mountain High" and "Aspenglow." Another favorite is "I Guess I'd Rather Be in Colorado."

Byron White was born in Fort Collins in 1917. He was the top student in his University of Colorado class. He also starred in sports. White played pro football before becoming a lawyer. In 1962, President John Kennedy named him to the U.S. Supreme Court. White served on the country's highest court until 1993.

Malcolm Scott Carpenter was born in Boulder in 1925. Carpenter served as a navy pilot. Later, he became an astronaut. In 1962, he became the second American to orbit the earth.

Patricia Schroeder was born in Oregon in 1940. She moved to Denver after she got married. For a few years, she worked as a lawyer. She also taught at Denver colleges. Then, in 1972, Schroeder ran for U.S. Congress and won. She became Colorado's first woman in Congress. By 1993, Schroeder had held office for twenty years.

The birthplace of Dr. Florence Sabin, Malcolm Scott Carpenter, Jack Dempsey, and Byron White . . .

Scott Carpenter

Home also to Black Kettle, Chipeta, Barney Ford, John Denver, and Patricia Schroeder . . .

The site of Pikes Peak, Royal Gorge, and the country's tallest sand dunes . . .

Today, a big producer of scientific equipment, beef cattle, horses, and wheat . . .

This is Colorado—the Centennial State.

Did You Know?

The largest silver nugget ever discovered in the United States was found at Aspen in 1894. It weighed about 1,840 pounds.

A Brachiosaurus skeleton found in Colorado belonged to one of the largest known dinosaurs. When alive, it weighed about 120,000 pounds.

Miners used to eat a yellow meat stew they called slumgullion. Southwest Colorado has an area where the soil is sticky, yellowish, and smelly due to landslides long ago. The region was named Slumgullion Slide for the old miners' stew.

Tiny Town is a miniature village near Denver. George Turner began it in 1915 for his daughter. Tiny Town's homes, churches, schools, and other buildings are about one-sixth of normal size.

Horace Tabor once owned about 7,200 square miles of southern Colorado. The states of Rhode Island and Connecticut together are smaller.

Ruth Handler of Denver invented the Barbie doll. Barbie is the world's most popular doll. Over a billion Barbies have been sold.

In 1893, Colorado became the second state to grant women the vote. Wyoming had done this in 1890. Women didn't gain full voting rights in most of the United States until 1920.

The road that climbs 14,264-foot Mt. Evans is the country's highest paved road.

In 1931, a school bus was stuck in a blizzard near Towner. The driver and five children died from the cold. Student Bryan Unteidt saved the other children by having them exercise to keep warm. President Herbert Hoover honored Unteidt at the White House.

Colorado has towns named Fruitvale, Gunbarrel, Parachute, Rifle, and Wild Horse.

Beans that Anasazi Indians left behind have been found in southwest Colorado. Usually 700-year-old food shouldn't be eaten. But the region's dryness preserved these nutritious beans. When planted, they grow. In 1983, Coloradans Ernie Waller and Bruce Riddell founded Adobe Milling. Their company sells Anasazi beans to stores.

Colorado has scenic areas with unusual shapes. Rabbit Ears Pass looks like the tall ears of a rabbit. Book Cliff looks like a row of huge books.

In 1987 Guffey, Colorado, elected a cat named Paisley as mayor. This town of about twenty-six people has had a cat as mayor ever since. Whiffey le Gone took office in 1991.

COLORADO INFORMATION

State flag

Columbine

Bighorn sheep

Area: 104,091 square miles (the eighth biggest state)

Greatest Distance North to South: 275 miles

Greatest Distance East to West: 385 miles

Border States: Wyoming to the north; Nebraska to the north and east; Kansas to the east; Oklahoma and New Mexico to the south; Arizona to the southwest; Utah to the west

Average Height of Colorado Land: 6,800 feet above sea level (the highest of the fifty states)

Highest Point: Mount Elbert, 14,433 feet above sea level

Lowest Point: 3,350 feet above sea level (along the Arkansas River in Prowers County)

Hottest Recorded Temperature: 118° F. (at Bennett, east of Denver, on July 11, 1888)

Coldest Recorded Temperature: -61° F. (at Maybell, in northwest Colorado on February 1, 1985)

Statehood: The thirty-eighth state, on August 1, 1876

Origin of Name: *Colorado* is a Spanish word meaning "red"; Colorado was named for the Colorado River, which flows through red canyons

Capital: Denver

Counties: 63

United States Representatives: 6 (as of 1992)

State Senators: 35

State Representatives: 65

State Song: "Where the Columbines Grow," by Arthur J. Flynn

State Motto: *Nil sine Numine,* Latin meaning "Nothing without Providence" ("Providence" means God or God's guidance)

Nickname: "Centennial State"

State Seal: Adopted in 1877

State Flag: Adopted in 1911

State Flower: Rocky Mountain columbine

State Bird: Lark bunting

State Tree: Blue spruce

State Animal: Rocky Mountain bighorn sheep

State Fossil: Stegosaurus

State Gemstone: Aquamarine

Lark bunting

Some Rivers: Colorado, Rio Grande, Arkansas, North Platte, South Platte, San Juan, Gunnison, Dolores

Some Lakes: Grand Lake, John Martin Reservoir, Blue Mesa Reservoir, Green Mountain Reservoir

Wildlife: Bighorn sheep, mountain goats, mountain lions, deer, elk, black bears, beavers, foxes, coyotes, prairie dogs, marmots, Colorado chipmunks, bobcats, pronghorn antelopes, lark buntings, owls, eagles, falcons, hawks, hummingbirds, many other kinds of birds, rattlesnakes, black widow spiders, trout, perch, catfish, bass, many other kinds of fish

Manufactured Products: Rockets, spacecraft, medical supplies, other scientific equipment, meats and other foods, beer and soft drinks, computers and office equipment, television cameras and other electrical equipment, greeting cards, luggage, clothing, lumber and furniture, books, pottery, sporting goods

Farm Products: Beef cattle, sheep, horses and ponies, milk, lettuce, cherries, pears, plums, potatoes, dry beans, barley, wheat, sugar beets, hay, corn, cucumbers, tomatoes, watermelons, apples, peaches

Mining Products: Oil, natural gas, coal, gold, silver, uranium, molybdenum

Population: 3,294,394, twenty-sixth among the fifty states (1990 U.S. Census Bureau figures)

Largest Cities (1990 Census):

Denver	467,610	Arvada	89,235
Colorado Springs	281,140	Fort Collins	87,758
Aurora	222,103	Boulder	83,312
Lakewood	126,481	Westminster	74,625
Pueblo	98,640	Greeley	60,536

Blue spruce

Colorado History

Colorado trapper Jim Baker

About 18,000 B.C.—Indians reach Colorado

About A.D. 1—Basket Maker Indians live in Colorado

About 400—Anasazi Indians reach Colorado

About 1200—The Anasazi build cliff dwellings in Colorado

About 1300—The Anasazi abandon Colorado

1598—Spaniard Juan de Oñate enters Colorado

1682—French explorer La Salle claims much of Colorado for France

1706—Juan de Ulibarri claims Colorado for Spain

1761—Juan Maria Rivera leads a Spanish expedition into Colorado in search of silver and gold

1803—Eastern Colorado becomes part of the United States through the Louisiana Purchase from France

1806—Zebulon Pike reaches Colorado

1820—Stephen H. Long explores Colorado; Dr. Edwin James leads the first-known successful climb up Pikes Peak

1821—Spain's claim to western Colorado passes to Mexico

1833—Colorado's first permanent non-Indian settlement, Bent's Fort, is built

1842—Jim Beckwourth helps found a trading post at Pueblo

1848—By the treaty ending the Mexican War, western Colorado comes under U.S. control

1858—Gold is discovered, setting off the Colorado gold rush

1861—The Colorado Territory is created by the U.S. Congress

1867—Denver becomes Colorado's capital

1870—Railroads reach Colorado

1876—Colorado becomes the thirty-eighth state on August 1

1878—Rich silver strikes are made in Colorado

1891—Cowboy Bob Womack finds gold in a pasture near the present town of Cripple Creek

1893—The price of silver drops, hurting Colorado's silver mining; Colorado becomes the second state (after Wyoming) to allow women to vote

1906—The U.S. Mint at Denver makes its first coins

1917-18—After the United States enters World War I, about 43,000 Coloradans serve

1929-39—The Great Depression and drought hurt Colorado

1941-45—After the United States enters World War II, almost 140,000 Colorado men and women serve

1959—The Colorado-Big Thompson Irrigation Project is completed

1962—Byron White becomes the first Coloradan on the U.S. Supreme Court

1966—The North American Aerospace Defense Command (NORAD) completes its command center within Cheyenne Mountain

1973—The world's highest road tunnel, the Eisenhower Memorial Tunnel, opens near Denver; Patricia Schroeder becomes the first Colorado woman in the U.S. House of Representatives

1976—The Big Thompson River floods and kills 139 people; the Centennial State is 100 years old

1983—Federico Peña becomes Denver's first Hispanic mayor

1985—The Frying Pan-Arkansas River Project is completed, bringing water to eastern Colorado

1991—Wellington Webb is elected Denver's first black mayor

1992—Ben Nighthorse Campbell is the second American Indian to be elected to the U.S. Senate

1993—The Colorado Rockies begin playing major-league baseball in Denver

The NORAD command center in Cheyenne Mountain

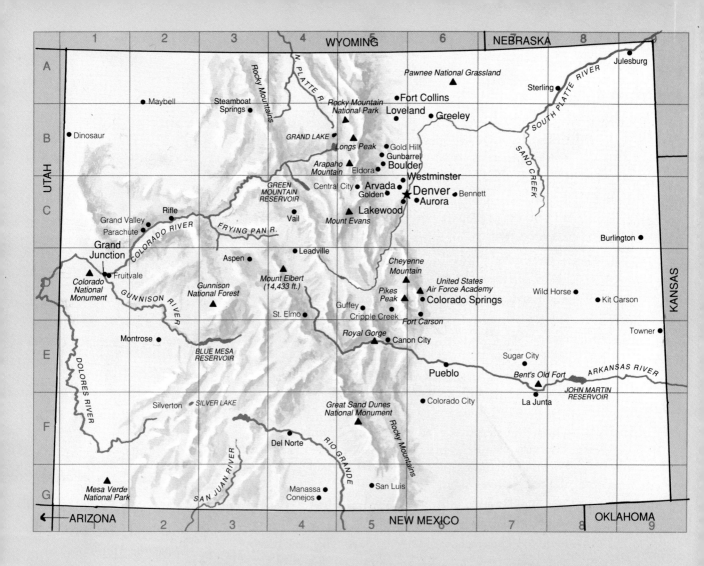

MAP KEY

GLOSSARY

ancient: Relating to a time early in history

artificial: Not occurring naturally; made by people

astronaut: A person who is highly trained for spaceflight

billion: A thousand million (1,000,000,000)

butte: A steep hill that towers over the nearby countryside

canyon: A deep, steep-sided valley

capital: A city that is the seat of government

capitol: The building in which the government meets

centennial: A 100th birthday or anniversary

climate: The typical weather of a region

dinosaur: A generally huge animal that died out millions of years ago

drought: A period when rainfall is well below normal in an area

explorer: A person who visits and studies unknown lands

fossils: The remains of animals or plants that lived long ago

ghost town: A town that still has buildings but few or no people

Hispanic: A person of Spanish-speaking background

irrigation: The watering of land through canals and other artificial means

manufacturing: The making of products

million: A thousand thousand (1,000,000)

permanent: Lasting

pioneer: A person who is among the first to move into a region

plain: Level or rolling, treeless land

pollution: The harming or dirtying of the environment

population: The number of people in a place

reservation: Land in the United States that is set aside for American Indians to live on

reservoir: A man-made lake where water is stored

ABOUT THE AUTHOR

Dennis Brindell Fradin is the author of 150 published children's books. His works for Childrens Press include the Young People's Stories of Our States series, the Disaster! series, and the Thirteen Colonies series. Dennis is married to Judith Bloom Fradin, who taught high-school and college English for many years. She is now Dennis's chief researcher. The Fradins are the parents of two sons, Anthony and Michael, and a daughter, Diana. Dennis graduated from Northwestern University in 1967 with a B.A. in creative writing, and has lived in Evanston, Illinois, since that year.